BEST
DIPS,
APPS, &
SIDES

BEST
DIPS,
APPS, &
SIDES

BUDGET-PROOF SNACKS, SPREADS, AND SIDE DISHES

MONICA SWEENEY

BEST DIPS, APPS, & SIDES

CONTENTS

INTRODUCTION / 7

Chapter One: Dips, Breads, & Bite-Sized Treats / 9

Classic Hummus

Guacamole

Cheesy Garlic Artichoke Dip

Adobo Salsa

Spinach & Bacon Dip

Savory Sausage Puffs

Spicy Fried Pickles

Stuffed Mushrooms

Honeydew & Prosciutto

Cucumbers & Tomatoes

Spinach Tart

Mini Margherita Pizzas

Chicken Empanadas

Sesame Breadsticks

Savory Pinwheels

Chapter Two: Hearty Eats / 41

Classic Chicken Wings

Lime & Chili Chicken Kebabs

Fiery Meatballs

Spicy Sliders

Beef Lettuce Wraps

Lamb Lollipops

Potato Skins

Lemon-Ginger Shrimp

Crab Cakes

Chapter Three: Salads & Veggies / 61

Kohlrabi Slaw

Beet & Arugula Salad

Caprese Salad

Vegetable Orzo Pasta Salad

Cous Cous Salad

Lemony Asparagus

Garlicky Green Beans

Creamed Spinach

Roasted Vegetable Medley

Balsamic Brussels Sprouts

Pine Nut Broccoli Rabe

Grilled Mexican Corn

Bok Choy

Walnut Carrots

Roasted Artichoke

Chapter Four: Pasta, Potatoes, Classic Casseroles, & More / 93

Mushroom Risotto

Orecchiette with Peas

Colby Jack Macaroni and
    Cheese

Crispy Potato Pancakes

Spicy Jicama Fries

Thyme Sweet Potatoes

Potato Gratin

Tortilla Española

Tomatoes Provencal

Baked Beans

Popovers

Zucchini Casserole

Cheesy Cauliflower

Rosemary Crispy Onions

Broccoli Quiche

INDEX / 124

Introduction

Whether you're hosting a party, attending a potluck, or just trying to put food on the table, it can be easy to fall into a tired routine of cooking the same thing time and again. Sometimes a home cook needs a little more inspiration than riffling through the recipe box.

The array of recipes in this book runs the gamut: from incredibly simple arrangements bursting with fresh flavor using but a few ingredients to more sophisticated medleys of spices, techniques, and ingredients that lead to incomparable taste. You will discover with every page turn that these dishes take your cooking from autumn and winter—with warming comfort foods that make every scrumptious bite feel like home—to spring and summer— with savory treats and hors d'oeuvres made with crisp fresh vegetables and zesty spices—perfect for a picnic or backyard gathering. Whatever the season or occasion, you're sure to find new ideas to perk up your menu.

This book takes dinner to the next level, whether for a large celebration or a quiet weeknight meal. Try these recipes out on your family, friends, or merely yourself and watch how your dips, apps, and sides can be as good as the main event.

CHAPTER ONE

DIPS, BREADS, & BITE-SIZED TREATS

Classic Hummus

There are few comforts greater than hummus with pita chips and veggies. Just a quick spin in the food processor and this snack can be yours! A healthy dip with endless potential, try tossing a handful of roasted red peppers or a seeded jalapeño in with the base ingredients to amplify the flavor power of this crudité staple.

Yield: about 2½ cups

2 cups canned chickpeas, drained

3 garlic cloves, peeled and minced

⅓ cup tahini sesame paste

Juice of 2 lemons

1½ tablespoons salt

2 tablespoons water

Pinch of paprika

1 teaspoon extra-virgin olive oil

Combine all ingredients except the paprika and olive oil into a food processor. Mix until pureed, stopping once or twice to scrape the sides and reincorporate with the mixture. Sprinkle with paprika and a dash of olive oil upon serving.

"At a dinner party one should eat wisely but not too well, and talk well but not too wisely."
—W. Somerset Maugham

Guacamole

Avocados may be the closest thing to produce perfection. This recipe puts its focus on the delicious, fresh, and flavor-packed ingredients like tangy lime, fiery jalapeños, and zesty cilantro that make guacamole taste so great. It will be sure to please as a stand-alone dip with corn chips, but this guacamole can play a leading role in other recipes, from omelets to hearty sandwiches.

Yield: 2 servings

Juice of 1 lime

3 avocados, peeled and halved

½ teaspoon salt

½ teaspoon ground cumin

½ teaspoon cayenne pepper

½ medium onion, diced

½ jalapeño pepper, seeded and minced

2 Roma tomatoes, seeded and diced

1 tablespoon chopped cilantro

1 clove garlic, minced

Set aside 1 tablespoon of lime juice and add the rest to a bowl with the avocados. Coat evenly, and then add the salt, cumin, and cayenne pepper. Mash with a fork or potato masher until blended. Fold in the remaining ingredients, including the lime juice, until mixed evenly. Serve at room temperature.

Cheesy Garlic Artichoke Dip

This hot and tasty dip is packed with delicious garlic flavor and just the right amount of artichokes to add taste and texture. Served with pita bread, chips, or raw vegetables, this dip ranks high on the list of best comfort foods.

Yield: 3 cups

1 head garlic

2 tablespoons extra-virgin olive oil

1 12-ounce jar artichoke hearts, drained

4 ounces cream cheese

½ cup sour cream or yogurt

¼ cup mayonnaise

¼ cup green onion, chopped

½ teaspoon freshly ground black pepper

1½ cups shredded cheese

Preheat the oven to 425°F. Slice off the top of a head of garlic, exposing the cloves inside. Place in foil and drizzle the olive oil over the garlic. Close the top of the foil over the head of garlic and place on a baking sheet. Cook for 30 minutes. Remove from the oven and let cool. Peel the outside skin of the garlic and remove the cloves. Reduce the oven temperature to 350°F. In a bowl, crush the garlic cloves into a paste. Chop the artichoke hearts into small chunks. In a large bowl, mix all ingredients together, reserving ½ cup of shredded cheese. Scoop the mixture into a baking dish and sprinkle the top with the remaining cheese. Bake for 35 minutes, broiling in the last 3 to 5 minutes to brown the top.

Adobo Salsa

This blend of fresh vegetables and hot peppers makes one fiery salsa. For those who prefer a little less spice, swap some of the hot peppers for sweet fruit like mango or pineapple.

Yield: 6–8 servings

1 14-ounce can fire-roasted tomatoes

1 cup fresh cherry tomatoes, sliced in half

½ cup white onion, chopped

2 cloves garlic, chopped

½ jalapeño, chopped and seeded

¼ cup chopped red onion

2 chipotle peppers in adobo

1 teaspoon adobo sauce

Pinch of salt and freshly ground black pepper

½ cup cilantro

Juice of 1 lime

Combine all of the ingredients in a food processor or high-powered blender and pulse until chunky.

Spinach & Bacon Dip

This hot and cheesy dip is more than just your typical spinach dip. With added bacon and spicy jalapeños, this is fondue turned fiery. Use it as a dip for chips, soft French bread, and vegetables for a savory snack that is sure to be a crowd-pleaser.

Yield: 8–10 servings

1 package fresh baby spinach

16 ounces Velveeta, cut into cubes

4 ounces cream cheese, softened

1 can diced tomatoes, drained

1 jalapeño

8 slices cooked bacon, broken into bits

Combine all of the ingredients into a microwaveable bowl. Microwave on high for 5 minutes or until cheese blend is completely melted. Stop halfway through to stir.

"Life is too short for self-hatred and celery sticks."

—Marilyn Wann

Savory Sausage Puffs

These delicious pastries are hard to put down. The best part of this recipe is that you can feel free to be creative with the variety of sausages you choose for each batch. Whether it's a sweet chicken-apple sausage or a spicy pork sausage, these sausage rolls bring out bold flavors with every bite.

Yield: 6–8 servings

½ pound sausage, removed from casing

¼ teaspoon dried basil

¼ teaspoon dried oregano

1 sheet pre-made puff pastry

Preheat the oven to 400°F. Mix sausage and spices. Unroll the puff pastry onto a floured surface. Using a pizza cutter, slice the pastry into three even sections. Roll out long tubes of sausage to fit the length of each section of puff pastry. Fold the puff pastry neatly over the sausage, pressing to seal the edges. Using a pizza cutter, slice the pastry tubes into 1-inch (bite-sized) portions and place them open-face down on a baking sheet. Bake for 15 minutes or until cooked through.

"Humor keeps us alive. Humor and food. Don't forget food. You can go a week without laughing."
—Joss Whedon

Spicy Fried Pickles

There are two fried pickle camps: spears or slices. From where I'm standing, slices reign supreme because of the great balance of hot pickle to flaky crust. Whichever way you choose to fry them up, these are by far the best bar snack that you can bring home.

Yield: 6–8 servings

4 cups vegetable oil

⅓ cup yellow cornmeal

⅔ cup all-purpose flour

2 teaspoons garlic powder

3 teaspoons paprika

1 teaspoon cayenne pepper

½ teaspoon cumin

1 16-ounce jar of dill pickles, drained and patted dry

½ cup banana peppers

Heat oil to 375°F in a deep stock pot. On a plate or in a shallow bowl, mix together the dry ingredients until evenly blended. Coat the pickles and peppers in the mixture until covered completely. Using a spider strainer or metal tongs, carefully lower 10 to 15 of the pickles and peppers into the hot oil. Let cook for 2 to 3 minutes or until golden brown. Remove the pickles and peppers using the spider strainer or metal tongs. Place them on a cooling rack or plate lined with paper towels to soak up the excess oil prior to serving.

"One cannot have too large a party."

—Jane Austen

Stuffed Mushrooms

Mushrooms stuffed with buttery breadcrumbs are nothing short of perfection. This particular recipe is vegetarian, but carnivores may want to add crunchy bacon to the tops of each mushroom for an extra element of flavor.

Yield: 10–12 servings

3 (8-ounce) packages button mushrooms

1 stick butter

½ cup Italian breadcrumbs

¼ teaspoon ground rosemary

Pinch of salt and freshly ground pepper

1 tablespoon green onion, chopped

Juice and zest of 1 lemon

Wash the mushrooms and remove the stems. Set 10 stems aside and discard the rest. Let the mushrooms dry for a couple of hours or overnight. Preheat the oven to 400°F. Melt the butter and chop up the mushroom stems. Combine breadcrumbs, rosemary, salt, pepper, and green onion in a bowl until blended. Add 1 tablespoon of lemon juice. Add more breadcrumbs if the mixture is too wet. Arrange the mushroom caps cavity-side up on a baking sheet. Spoon the mixture into the caps until full. Cook for 40 minutes.

Honeydew & Prosciutto

The underappreciated member of the melon family, honeydew takes center stage in this spin on the traditional cantaloupe wrapped in prosciutto recipe. The blend of juicy, fresh fruit and savory prosciutto will become the new standard.

Yield: 20–25 honeydew balls

1 honeydew melon

12 slices prosciutto

Slice the honeydew in half, removing the seeds. Using a melon baller, firmly press into the flesh of the melon and twist to form ball shape. Continue forming melon balls until the melon has been cleaned. Tear prosciutto into manageable pieces and wrap around the melon balls. Place seam-facedown on serving platter or secure with toothpicks.

"One cannot think well, love well, sleep well, if one has not dined well."
—Virginia Woolf

Cucumbers & Tomatoes

These bite-sized appetizers bring raw vegetables and dip to a new playing field. The refreshing cucumber and creamy dill spread are just the right size, and the sun-dried tomatoes bring in bold flavor.

Yield: 15–20 slices

1 (8-ounce) package cream cheese, softened

1 teaspoon dried dill weed

1 teaspoon dried tarragon

¼ cup mayonnaise

½ teaspoon garlic powder

Pinch of salt and freshly ground black pepper

1 cucumber, sliced

12 sun-dried tomatoes

Blend the cream cheese, dill, tarragon, mayo, garlic powder, salt, and pepper in a food processor until smooth. Pour mixture into a pastry bag and pipe onto cucumber slices. Top with sun-dried tomatoes.

Spinach Tart

More than a pizza, this delicious snack combines the incredible flavors of caramelized onions, fresh greens, and cheese over a buttery pastry crust. It can be put together in no time, and offers incredible flavors for even the pickiest eaters.

Yield: 4 servings

1 puff pastry sheet

1 tablespoon olive oil

¼ cup fresh spinach

¼ cup Swiss chard

½ cup of caramelized onion

2 tablespoons fresh basil, chopped

1 medium-sized tomato, thinly sliced

½ cup shredded mozzarella cheese

¼ cup shredded Parmesan cheese

Preheat the oven to 400°F. Unroll the puff pastry onto a floured surface. Fold the edges of the pastry to form a ½-inch crust. Brush the puff pastry with olive oil and bake in the oven for 10 minutes. Remove from the oven and add the spinach, Swiss chard, caramelized onion, basil, sliced tomato, and sprinkle on the cheeses. Bake for another 10 minutes or so, or until the crust has browned and the cheese is bubbling.

"Before we begin our banquet, I would like to say a few words. And here they are: *Nitwit! Blubber! Oddment! Tweak!* Thank you."

—Albus Dumbledore

Mini Margherita Pizzas

A little something for everyone! These mini pizzas are great for large groups and incredibly simple to put together. The traditional Margherita never fails, but additional ingredients like bacon or prosciutto can add an extra layer of flavor to this great snack.

Yield: 15–20 mini pizzas

1 12-inch thin-crust pizza crust

½ cup marinara sauce

6 ounces fresh mozzarella cheese, sliced

2 Roma tomatoes, thinly sliced

1 tablespoon crushed red pepper

6–8 fresh basil leaves

1 tablespoon Parmesan, powdered

Preheat oven to 450°F. Using a 2-inch metal cookie cutter, press out 15 to 20 circles from pizza crust. If you do not have a cookie cutter, slice crust into squares with a pizza cutter or knife. Arrange mini pizza crusts onto a foil-lined baking sheet. Top with marinara sauce, sliced mozzarella, and sliced tomatoes. Bake for 8 to 10 minutes or until cheese is bubbling. Finish with crushed red pepper, fresh basil, and a sprinkle of Parmesan.

Chicken Empanadas

The father of all hand pies, the chicken empanada has just the right amount of spice and is endlessly satisfying. Incredible on their own, these empanadas will be an instant crowd-pleaser with the addition of Oaxaca cheese or a spicy chipotle mayo.

Yield: 6–8 servings

1 cup chicken, cooked and shredded

½ cup cheddar cheese, grated

½ cup Monterey jack cheese, grated

3 tablespoons green onions, minced

1 can green chili, chopped

1 teaspoon minced garlic

½ teaspoon dried cilantro

½ teaspoon cumin, ground

½ teaspoon paprika

Pinch of salt and freshly ground black pepper

2 sheets pie pastry

3 egg yolks

2 tablespoons kosher salt

1 tablespoon chili powder

Preheat the oven to 400°F. In a bowl, combine the chicken, cheeses, green onions, green chili, garlic, cilantro, spices, salt, and pepper. Unroll the pie pastry onto a lightly floured surface. Using a 4-inch cookie cutter or overturned glass, cut out pastry circles until all of the dough has been used. Spoon 2 tablespoons of the combined ingredients onto the center of the pie pastries. Fold the pie pastry neatly over the meat, pressing to seal the edges.

Crimp with fork if desired. Arrange the empanadas evenly on a baking sheet. Brush with egg yolks, then sprinkle with a mixture of the salt and chili powder. Bake for 12 to 14 minutes or until golden brown.

"My doctor told me I had to stop having intimate dinners for four unless there are three other people."

—Orson Welles

Sesame Breadsticks

When hunger pangs strike, reach for the breadsticks. These crunchy spears are coated with sesame seeds for an extra element of texture and are great on their own or paired with an Italian dinner.

Yield: 15–18 breadsticks

1 cup warm water, divided

1 teaspoon honey

1 envelope active dry yeast

1½ cups bread flour

1½ cups all-purpose flour

1 teaspoon sugar

1 teaspoon salt

2 tablespoons sesame oil

Cornmeal for sprinkling

1 egg, beaten with 1 tablespoon water for egg wash

¼ cup sesame seeds, toasted

Prepare a ¼ cup of warm water and stir in honey. Add the yeast and let rest for 5 to 10 minutes or until foamy. In a large bowl, mix together the flours, sugar, and salt. Add the yeast mixture, sesame oil, and remaining warm water and stir together. On a lightly floured surface, knead the dough for about 10 minutes or until smooth. Place the dough in a lightly greased bowl and cover with a damp towel. Let rise until doubled, about 1 hour. Press down the dough and allow to rest for another 5 minutes. Roll out the dough on a lightly floured surface. Shape into a large rectangle. Using a pizza cutter, slice the dough into long strips about 1 inch wide. Arrange the breadsticks onto baking sheets sprinkled with cornmeal. Brush with egg wash and sprinkle

with sesame seeds. Cover with a damp towel and let rise for another hour. While the dough is rising, preheat the oven to 425°F. Bake for 15 minutes or until crunchy.

Savory Pinwheels

These little pastries are fun additions to any gathering. With such great elements as goat cheese, spinach, bacon, herbs, and spices, these buttery pinwheels will be an instant favorite.

Yield: 6–8 servings

1 sheet puff pastry

5 ounces goat cheese

⅛ teaspoon garlic powder

Pinch of salt and freshly ground black pepper

¼ cup green onions, chopped

5 slices bacon, crisp and broken into pieces

1½ cups fresh spinach, chopped

Preheat the oven to 350°F. Unroll the pastry dough and divide into 2 long rectangles. Spread the goat cheese onto the dough and then top with garlic powder, salt, pepper, green onions, bacon, and spinach. Roll the dough up like a jellyroll, pressing the edges together at the end to seal. Divide the roll into 6 to 8 slices and arrange the slices evenly onto an ungreased cookie sheet. Do this for both rectangles. Bake for 15 minutes or until the dough is golden brown.

"If you really want to make a friend, go to someone's house and eat with him . . . the people who give you their food give you their heart."

—Cesar Chavez

CHAPTER TWO

HEARTY EATS

Classic Chicken Wings

From meat-and-potatoes lovers to refined foodies, chicken wings are the appetizer go-to loved by all. This classic marinade is as easy to make as it is delicious. Whether you're preparing for a tailgate party or just have a craving for some good old-fashioned wings, this simple recipe will have everyone in your crowd raving.

Yield: 6–8 servings

2 tablespoons all-purpose flour

1 teaspoon salt

¼ teaspoon pepper

¼ teaspoon garlic powder

1 tablespoon Old Bay seasoning

2 pounds chicken wingettes and drumettes

2½ tablespoons hot sauce

2 tablespoons unsalted butter, melted

2 tablespoons Worcestershire sauce

Preheat the oven to 500°F. In a bowl, mix the flour, salt, pepper, garlic powder, and Old Bay seasoning. Coat the chicken evenly. Arrange the chicken on a parchment or foil-lined baking sheet without overlapping. Cook for 45 minutes or until crispy, turning the chicken midway through with tongs. While the chicken cooks, whisk the hot sauce, butter, and Worcestershire sauce together. Remove the chicken from the oven and use tongs to dunk the pieces in the sauce, coating evenly.

"And I like large parties. They're so intimate. At small parties there isn't any privacy."　　　　　　　　　　—F. Scott Fitzgerald, *The Great Gatsby*

Lime & Chili
Chicken Kebabs

Nothing says summer like lightly charred kebabs fresh off the grill. The spices and citrus add a delightful zing to complement most anything you decide to put on your kebabs, from chicken, pineapple, onion, and peppers, to bites of summer squash and zucchini. This recipe makes putting meat and vegetables on a stick taste like a culinary masterpiece.

Yield: 4 servings

3 tablespoons olive oil

1½ tablespoons red wine vinegar

Juice of 1 lime

½ teaspoon chili powder

½ teaspoon paprika

½ teaspoon onion powder

½ teaspoon garlic powder

1 teaspoon dried cilantro

1 teaspoon Sriracha

1 teaspoon cayenne pepper

Pinch of salt and freshly ground black pepper

1 pound skinless, boneless chicken thighs

Combine all ingredients except chicken in a mixing bowl and whisk until completely blended. Cut chicken into 1½ inch pieces. Arrange the chicken in a shallow baking dish and coat with sauce. Cover and let marinate in the refrigerator for one hour at minimum. Preheat the grill to medium-high. Lightly grease just before using. Thread chicken onto skewers and grill 10 to 15 minutes or until cooked through. If using wooden skewers, presoak them in water for 20 minutes before using.

Fiery Meatballs

The sauce makes this recipe. Whether you swear by making meatballs from scratch or prefer the ease of the store-bought variety, the delicious blend of smoky spices and savory beef stock bring out the best in this well-loved party staple.

Yield: About 25 meatballs

2 tablespoons salted butter

¼ cup all-purpose flour

1 cup beef broth

¾ cup A1 steak sauce

½ cup chili sauce

½ cup ketchup

2 tablespoons Worcestershire sauce

1 teaspoon hot pepper sauce

1 package or 25 small meatballs

In a large saucepan, melt butter on a medium to high heat. Add flour and stir until light brown to make a roux. Add beef broth and stir until thickened. Add the remaining ingredients, adding the meatballs last. Keep pan covered except to stir occasionally. Cook for 15 to 20 minutes or until heated through.

"I am not a glutton. I am an explorer of food."

—Erma Bombeck

Spicy Sliders

These sliders are straightforward to make but have tons of flavor. While store-bought sliders are certainly available, mixing up some fresh ground beef and savory ingredients is a simple way to make some of the best tasting juicy burgers around. The slider-style size is fantastic for serving large groups, but this recipe can also go large scale with full-sized burgers.

Yield: 10 sliders

1 pound ground sirloin

1 medium onion, diced

2 tablespoons Worcestershire sauce

1 tablespoon red hot sauce

¼ teaspoon garlic powder

Pinch of salt and freshly ground black pepper

10 small slices cheddar cheese

10 slider buns, toasted

10 small lettuce leaves, any type, for serving

2 Roma or plum tomatoes, thinly sliced crosswise, for serving

Mix ground sirloin with onion, Worcestershire sauce, hot sauce, garlic powder, salt, and pepper. Scoop into small patties (about two tablespoons) and arrange on a parchment-lined baking sheet. Preheat broiler and broil for 4 to 5 minutes. Top burgers with cheese just before removing from the oven. Plate with slider buns, lettuce, tomato, and any additional toppings of your choice.

Beef Lettuce Wraps

These lettuce wraps are a delectable and healthy alternative to many typical appetizers. The blend of ingredients is crunchy and zesty, and the beef can be swapped with other proteins like chicken, shrimp, and even tofu.

Yield: 4 servings

1 teaspoon vegetable oil

1 pound ground beef

2 teaspoons ginger, minced

2 scallions, chopped

2 cloves garlic, minced

2 tablespoons soy sauce

1 teaspoon sesame oil

1 teaspoon red pepper flakes

¼ cup water chestnuts

¼ cup hoisin sauce

¼ cup chopped peanuts

Salt and freshly ground black pepper

1 head Bibb lettuce

Heat oil at medium-high heat in a large sauté pan. Add beef and cook until browned, and then add the ginger, scallions, garlic, soy sauce, sesame oil, red pepper flakes, water chestnuts, and hoisin. Stir for another minute and remove from the heat. Fold in the peanuts and sprinkle with salt and pepper. Scoop spoonfuls into the lettuce and serve immediately.

Lamb Lollipops

Just big enough to stave off hunger but not so big that they'll take away from the main course, these juicy lamb chops are the perfect appetizer size. Great on the grill or sautéed, the hint of rosemary and garlic adds all the flavor you'll need.

Yield: 6 lamb lollipops

5 tablespoons extra-virgin olive oil, divided

½ cup red wine

1 tablespoon rosemary leaves

1 teaspoon garlic, minced

Pinch of salt and freshly ground black pepper

6 double lamb rib chops (4 ounces each)

2 rosemary sprigs

Preheat the oven to 400°F. Combine 3 tablespoons olive oil, red wine, rosemary, and garlic in a small bowl and set aside. Heat 2 tablespoons of oil in a large, oven-safe sauté pan over medium-high. Sprinkle the lamb with salt and pepper and then lay flat in the pan. Sear the lamb for 2 to 3 minutes, or until the meat has browned. Turn the lamb and cook for another 2 to 3 minutes, basting with the olive oil mixture throughout. Place the sauté pan in the oven and cook for another 5 minutes or until medium-rare. Plate and garnish with fresh rosemary.

"Always remember: If you're alone in the kitchen and you drop the lamb, you can always just pick it up. Who's going to know?"

—Julia Child

Potato Skins

This appetizer is a classic for a reason, perfect for game-day entertaining or as a hearty snack. For an extra kick, top with jalapeños or hot red sauce.

Yield: 8 servings

4 large baking potatoes

3 tablespoons vegetable oil

¼ teaspoon garlic powder

¼ teaspoon paprika

Pinch of salt and freshly ground black pepper

1 tablespoon grated Parmesan cheese

2 cups shredded Cheddar cheese

8 slices bacon, chopped into bits

Clean the potatoes and make perforations using a toothpick. Heat in the microwave for 12 to 14 minutes, stopping halfway through to turn and check for doneness. Once the potatoes have cooled, slice them in half, lengthwise. Scoop out the contents in the middle and discard. Heat 2 inches of vegetable oil in frying pan to 365°F. Mix remaining oil, garlic powder, paprika, salt, pepper, and Parmesan in a small bowl. Brush over skins. Fry the potato skins in batches for 5 minutes. Remove potato skins from the oil and set on a cooling rack or plate lined with paper towels to soak up excess oil. Preheat the oven to 450°F. Arrange potato skins facedown in a greased baking dish. Bake for 8 minutes. Flip the potato skins over and add cheese and bacon. Bake for 8 more minutes or until cheese has melted.

"What I say is that, if a man really likes potatoes, he must be a pretty decent sort of fellow."
—A. A. Milne

Lemon-Ginger Shrimp

This is shrimp cocktail with a personality. A perfect excuse for firing up the grill, lemon-ginger shrimp go great on skewers for kebabs, but are just as delicious plated all on their own. With the zesty flavors of lemon and ginger, these shrimp appetizers have the extra kick you're looking for.

Yield: 6–8 servings

2 teaspoons garlic, peeled and minced

2 tablespoons fresh ginger, minced

3 teaspoons sesame oil

1 tablespoon soy sauce

⅓ cup olive oil

2 tablespoons rice wine vinegar

Pinch of salt and freshly ground black pepper

2 pounds raw jumbo shrimp, peeled

2 tablespoons chives, chopped

Whisk the garlic, ginger, sesame oil, soy sauce, olive oil, rice wine vinegar, salt, and pepper together. Place cleaned shrimp in a bowl or storage container, and pour in the mixture. Cover and let marinate in the refrigerator for 30 minutes. If cooking on skewers, thread the two sides of the shrimp to form a C. Lightly oil the grill or a sauté pan, setting the heat on medium. Cook the shrimp for 2 to 3 minutes per side or until pink. Brush with extra marinade as they cook. Sprinkle with chives and serve.

Crab Cakes

Seafood lovers, unite! In just a few short steps, you can feel like you're on a beach-side boardwalk in no time. These crab cakes are big on flavor, from the fresh pieces of crab to the traditional tartar sauce.

Yield: 6 crab cakes

1 large egg

2½ tablespoons mayonnaise

1½ teaspoons Dijon mustard

1 teaspoon Worcestershire sauce

1 teaspoon Old Bay seasoning

¼ teaspoon salt

¼ cup celery, diced

2 cloves garlic, minced

¼ cup yellow onion, chopped

2 tablespoons fresh parsley, chopped

1 cup crabmeat

½ cup panko breadcrumbs

2 tablespoons vegetable oil for cooking

In a large bowl, combine all of the ingredients except the crabmeat, breadcrumbs, and vegetable oil. Once blended, fold in the crabmeat and the breadcrumbs. Shape the mixture into 6 large crabcakes, cover, and refrigerate for at least 1 hour. In a large saucepan, heat vegetable oil on medium-high. Cook the crabcakes in the saucepan for about 3 to 5 minutes on each side or until golden brown. Place on a cooling rack or plate lined with a paper towel to soak up the excess oil. Top with tartar sauce and serve with lemon wedges.

CHAPTER THREE

SALADS & VEGGIES

Kohlrabi Slaw

Coleslaw is often relegated to summer barbecues and as the tagalong of cornbread. This slaw uses fresh kohlrabi and a light, lemony vinaigrette instead of the standard sugary mayonnaise. If you can't find kohlrabi, try it with jicama, turnips, or another fresh and crisp vegetable.

Yield: 4–6 servings

1 cup kohlrabi, grated

1 cup carrots, grated

2 cups green cabbage, shredded

2 tablespoons lemon juice

3 tablespoons extra-virgin olive oil

½ tablespoon honey

½ tablespoon brown mustard

Pinch of salt and freshly ground black pepper

¼ cup scallions, sliced

Toss kohlrabi, carrots, and cabbage together in a large bowl. In a small bowl, make the dressing by whisking the lemon juice, olive oil, honey, mustard, salt, and pepper. Toss dressing with slaw, garnish with scallions, and serve chilled.

"There is no love sincerer than the love of food."

—George Bernard Shaw

Beet & Arugula Salad

Fresh, sweet beets and peppery arugula are the perfect match. With a light lemony dressing, crunchy walnuts, and creamy goat cheese, this salad has it all. Serve this salad as a side or top it with some protein for a whole meal.

Yield: 2 servings

3 medium beets

¼ cup balsamic vinegar

1 tablespoon lemon juice

3 tablespoons shallots, thinly sliced

1 tablespoon honey

⅓ cup extra-virgin olive oil

Salt and freshly ground black pepper

6 cups fresh arugula

½ cup walnuts, toasted, chopped

3 ounces goat cheese, crumbled

Preheat the oven to 450°F. Loosely wrap beets in foil and bake for 30 to 35 minutes and set aside to cool. Peel and cut into slices. Whisk the vinegar, lemon juice, shallots, and honey together in a bowl. Blend the oil in gradually and season with salt and pepper. Toss the arugula, walnuts, and beets with the dressing. Plate and top with goat cheese.

Caprese Salad

There is nothing like a fresh mozzarella, tomato, and basil salad. Made of fresh ingredients that instinctively belong together, you can prepare it in just about any manner and it will automatically come out incredible. Mix together this dressing and drizzle over the mozzarella and tomato for an undeniably beautiful salad.

Yield: 2 servings

1 lemon, juiced

1 tablespoon red wine vinegar

1 small clove garlic, minced

Pinch of salt and freshly ground black pepper

⅓ cup extra-virgin olive oil

1 cup fresh cherry tomatoes, halved

1 cup mozzarella pearls, drained

½ cup basil leaves

Whisk lemon juice, vinegar, garlic, salt, pepper, and olive oil together until evenly blended. Toss dressing with tomatoes and mozzarella. Garnish with basil leaves.

"First we eat, then we do everything else."

—M. F. K. Fisher

Vegetable Orzo Pasta Salad

Is your old pasta salad recipe due for an update? Put the elbow macaroni back into the cupboard and try this fresh-tasting recipe using orzo, crisp veggies, and fresh herbs. The homemade vinaigrette is a cinch, and your modern twist on this classic will be ready in no time!

Yield: 8 servings

¼ cup red wine vinegar

2 tablespoons fresh lemon juice

½ cup olive oil

¼ teaspoon oregano

¼ teaspoon garlic powder

Pinch of salt and freshly ground black pepper

6 cups chicken broth

1 pound orzo

2 cups grape tomatoes

1 cup broccoli florets, blanched

1½ cups feta cheese

½ cup Kalamata olives

1 cup fresh basil, chopped

1 cup chopped green onions

½ cup pine nuts, toasted

To make vinaigrette, whisk vinegar and lemon juice together in small bowl, slowly adding in oil. Season with oregano, garlic powder, salt, and pepper. In a large saucepan, bring broth to a boil. Add in orzo and lower heat to medium,

partially covered. Cook for 5 to 7 minutes, or until tender. Drain and toss until cool. Once cooled, add tomatoes, broccoli, feta, olives, basil, green onions, and pine nuts until blended evenly. Toss with vinaigrette and serve.

Cous Cous Salad

A bright and summery salad with the reviving flavors of pomegranate and lime, this is the medley to go along with fresh fish or grilled chicken. For a no-fuss way to remove the pomegranate seeds for this salad, halve and soak the fruit in water. After a few minutes, tap the peel vigorously with a wooden spoon over the bowl of water.

Yield: 8 servings

2 cups water

2 cups cous cous

⅓ cup extra-virgin olive oil

2 cloves garlic, minced

1 pomegranate, seeded

1 cup dried cranberries

½ cup mint leaves, chopped

½ cup parsley, chopped

2 tablespoons sesame seeds, toasted

Juice of 1 lime

Salt and pepper to taste

In a heat-safe bowl, pour boiling water over cous cous. Cover and let sit for 5 minutes while water absorbs. Fluff with fork and let cool. Toss with other ingredients and serve.

"Food is symbolic of love when words are inadequate."

—Alan D. Wolfelt

Lemony
Asparagus

Welcome in springtime with this simple asparagus dish you can toss together in minutes! Asparagus is a fantastic source of nutrients and vitamins and when sautéed with garlic and shallots and topped with Parmesan cheese, it's a stunning addition to your family table.

Yield: 2–4 servings

1 tablespoon olive oil

1 medium shallot, minced

1 clove garlic, minced

1 bunch fresh asparagus spears, trimmed

Juice of 1 lemon

Pinch of salt and freshly ground black pepper

¼ cup Parmesan cheese

Heat olive oil, shallots, and garlic on medium heat for about 1 minute or until aromatic. Add asparagus and cook for 5 minutes, or until tender and slightly browned. Remove from heat and season with lemon juice, salt, and pepper, and top with cheese.

Garlicky Green Beans

Crisp green beans can be served with nearly any meal, whether it's fresh and lemony seafood or a rosemary tenderloin. This recipe is modest because the garden-fresh flavor of green beans needs no frills to be absolutely delectable.

Yield: 4 servings

1 pound green beans

2 tablespoons extra-virgin olive oil

2 cloves garlic, sliced

Pinch of salt and freshly ground black pepper

½ teaspoon crushed red pepper

Boil water in a large saucepan, and then add the green beans. Cook for 3 to 4 minutes or until al dente. Strain and set aside. Heat olive oil and garlic on medium heat for about 1 minute or until aromatic. Add the green beans, salt, and black pepper and stir until combined and hot. Sprinkle with crushed red pepper and serve hot.

Creamed Spinach

Creamed spinach tends to go underappreciated, but it's a true side dish gem. While many people prepare this dish with frozen spinach and canned mushrooms and throw it in the oven, using fresh ingredients can be just as easy and the results are far superior. For some additional texture, add crispy onions to the top prior to serving.

Yield: 4 servings

2 packages (10 ounces each) fresh baby spinach

3–4 tablespoons salted butter

2 cloves garlic, minced

1 onion, diced

1 cup white mushrooms, sliced

3–4 tablespoons all-purpose flour

2 cups milk

½ cup grated Parmesan cheese

¼ teaspoon nutmeg

Pinch of salt and freshly ground black pepper

Blanch spinach in a pot of boiling water for 1 minute. Drain and transfer spinach to a bowl of cold water to stop the cooking process. Drain and squeeze excess water from the cooked spinach with a clean, dry kitchen towel. Chop the spinach and remove large stems. Set aside. Melt butter in a saucepan and add the garlic, onion, and mushrooms. Cook until tender or the onions are translucent. Stir in the flour until the mixture becomes a paste, then stir in the milk to thicken. Stir in the Parmesan, nutmeg, and then the spinach. Season with salt and pepper and serve.

"We all eat, and it would be a sad waste of opportunity to eat badly."
—Anna Thomas

Roasted
Vegetable Medley

Sprinkle your favorite vegetables with some rosemary, salt, freshly cracked pepper, and a drizzle of great olive oil for the most perfect expression of natural flavors. This no-frills recipe showcases just how simple, fresh ingredients can be equal to— if not better than—some of the most extravagant recipes.

Yield: 4–6 servings

½ head cauliflower

½ head broccoli

6 carrots, peeled

1 medium red onion, peeled and chopped

3 tablespoons extra-virgin olive oil

½ teaspoon dried rosemary

½ teaspoon oregano

2 teaspoons salt

1 teaspoon freshly ground black pepper

Preheat the oven to 400°F. Break cauliflower and broccoli down into florets. Discard larger stems. Cut large carrots into halves or quarters, lengthwise, and leave smaller carrots whole. Toss vegetables with olive oil, rosemary, oregano, salt, and pepper. Arrange in a cast-iron pan or on a parchment- or foil-lined baking sheet. Roast in the oven for 25 minutes, or until tender and slightly browned.

Balsamic Brussels Sprouts

You may remember the days when Brussels sprouts were typically boiled and served. These poor sprouts got a bad rap for being mushy and flavorless for too long. Thankfully times have changed in the kitchen and this side is not only packed with flavor, but Vitamin C and fiber, too!

Yield: 6 servings

1½ pounds Brussels sprouts

3 tablespoons extra-virgin olive oil, divided

Pinch of salt and freshly ground black pepper

Juice of 1 lemon

1 teaspoon honey

1 tablespoon balsamic vinegar

Preheat oven to 425°F. Cut off Brussels sprout bases and any wilting leaves. Slice into halves for smaller sprouts and quarters for larger sprouts. Toss the sprouts with 2 tablespoons olive oil, salt, and pepper. Arrange on a parchment- or foil-lined baking sheet and cook for 20 to 25 minutes, or until crispy. Place cooked sprouts in a bowl and toss with 1 tablespoon of olive oil, lemon juice, honey, and balsamic vinegar until dressed evenly.

"Food is everything we are. It's an extension of nationalist feeling, ethnic feeling, your personal history, your province, your region, your tribe, your grandma. It's inseparable from those from the get-go."   —Anthony Bourd

Pine Nut Broccoli Rabe

Sometimes known as rapini, broccoli rabe is the slightly peppery vegetable that has everything. With a little added crunch from the toasted pine nuts, this can go with just about any meal, from fresh-roasted fish to a hearty steak.

Yield: 4–6 servings

4 bunches broccoli rabe, stems trimmed

2 tablespoons pine nuts, toasted

¼ cup olive oil

3 garlic cloves, chopped

½ teaspoon crushed red pepper flakes

Pinch of salt and freshly ground black pepper

Blanch broccoli rabe in a pot of boiling water for 1 minute. Drain and transfer to a bowl of cold water to stop the cooking process, reserving ¼ cup of cooking water. Drain the broccoli rabe and set aside. In a pan or toaster oven, toast the pine nuts for 2 to 3 minutes or until lightly browned. Heat olive oil and garlic on medium heat for about 1 minute or until aromatic. Reduce to low heat and add broccoli rabe, stirring until mixed with garlic and oil. Add the cooking water and cook for 4 to 5 minutes or until tender. Toss with toasted pine nuts and red pepper flakes and season with salt and pepper prior to serving.

"He who distinguishes the true savor of his food can never be a glutton; he who does not cannot be otherwise."   —Henry David Thoreau

Grilled Mexican Corn

There's nothing like fresh, sweet corn in the summertime. While corn is delicious with some butter and salt, the added flavors of chili powder and tangy lime really give it extra star power.

Yield: 4 ears

4 ears corn

1 tablespoon salt

½ cup mayonnaise

1½ cups sour cream

½ teaspoon celery salt

¼ cup freshly chopped cilantro leaves

1 lime, juiced

1 cup freshly grated Parmesan (optional)

Red chili powder, to taste

Preheat the grill to medium. Pull down the cornhusks without detaching. Remove the silk and fold the husks back over the corn. Let sit in water with 1 tablespoon of salt for 10 minutes. Dry off the corn and grill for 15 to 20 minutes, turning periodically to cook all sides. Mix the mayonnaise, sour cream, celery salt, and cilantro. Remove the husks and lather the corn with the mayonnaise mixture. Squeeze lime juice over the corn and then sprinkle liberally with Parmesan, if using. Finish with chili powder and serve.

Bok Choy

Bok choy is perpetually given a supporting role to most dishes instead of the lead. This crisp, slightly bitter green is a delicious mealtime component, especially when prepared with the right blend of lively ingredients. With a little bit of ginger, soy sauce, and garlic, this tangy recipe brings out the very best aspects of this show-stopping veggie.

Yield: 4–6 servings

½ tablespoon olive oil

½ tablespoon sesame oil

1 tablespoon minced fresh ginger

2 cloves garlic, minced

1 tablespoon rice wine vinegar

4 heads bok choy, whole or chopped

2 tablespoons soy sauce

Pinch of salt and freshly ground black pepper

Heat olive oil, sesame oil, ginger, and garlic on medium heat for about 1 minute or until aromatic. Add vinegar, bok choy, and soy sauce, cooking for 5 minutes or until the greens have wilted. Season with salt and pepper to taste.

Walnut Carrots

There is no more perfect way to cook carrots than this simple recipe. With a little bit of salt to bring out their natural sweetness and chopped walnuts to add an extra crunch, these roasted carrots are sure to be a side dish staple.

Yield: 2 servings

12 carrots, peeled

3 tablespoons extra-virgin olive oil

2 teaspoons salt

1 teaspoon freshly ground black pepper

½ teaspoon dried thyme

½ cup chopped walnuts

Preheat the oven to 400°F. Cut large carrots into halves or quarters, lengthwise, and leave smaller carrots whole. Toss carrots with olive oil, salt, pepper, and thyme. Spread carrots out on a parchment- or foil-lined baking sheet. Roast in the oven for 25 minutes, or until tender and slightly browned. Sprinkle with thyme and chopped walnuts when ready to serve.

Roasted Artichoke

This roasted artichoke is simple and delicious, complemented by a little bit of lemon and a lot of garlic. Preparation involves very little effort, and the payoff is tenfold. For those who have never eaten an artichoke in whole form before, just tear off the leaves and scrape off the meaty bits with your teeth to enjoy a mouthwatering and healthy supplement to your meal.

Yield: 2 servings

2 artichokes

1 lemon

2 tablespoons extra-virgin olive oil

Pinch of salt and freshly ground black pepper

6 garlic cloves

Preheat oven to 425°F. Prepare the artichokes by cutting off the bottom stems and very tops. Hollow out the center leaves to make room for the garlic, and spread the rest of the leaves out. Squeeze half a lemon and drizzle 1 tablespoon of olive oil over each artichoke. Sprinkle with salt and pepper and fill the cavities with 3 garlic cloves each. Wrap artichokes individually with foil and roast for 1 hour, or until tender.

CHAPTER FOUR

PASTA, POTATOES, CLASSIC CASSEROLES, & MORE

Mushroom Risotto

This scrumptious risotto dish is nothing if not comforting. The Arborio rice is the benchmark for this recipe, but you can swap it out with barley and brown rice as well.

Yield: 6 servings

6 cups chicken broth

3 tablespoons olive oil, divided

1 cup Portobello mushrooms, thinly sliced

1 cup white mushrooms, thinly sliced

1 cup shiitake mushrooms, thinly sliced

2 shallots, diced

2 cloves garlic, minced

1½ cups Arborio rice

½ cup dry white wine

4 tablespoons butter

⅓ cup Parmesan, grated

3 tablespoons parsley, chopped

Pinch of salt and freshly ground black pepper

Warm the chicken broth in a saucepan over low heat. In a separate, large skillet, heat 2 tablespoons of olive oil over medium-high. Add the mushrooms to the same skillet, and cook for 2 to 3 minutes or until tender. Remove the mushrooms and set aside. Add another tablespoon of olive oil to the same skillet and then add the shallots and garlic. Cook until warmed, and then slowly stir in the rice for about 2 minutes. Pour in white wine, stirring to coat the rice evenly until absorbed. Ladle in chicken broth ½ cup at a time, stirring constantly. Wait until each addition is absorbed before ladling in more. After 15 to 20 minutes when all the broth is fully absorbed, remove the risotto from the burner. Fold in mushrooms, butter, and Parmesan. Garnish with parsley and sprinkle with salt and pepper.

Orecchiette with Peas

Orecchiette comes from the Italian word for "little ears," which is a cute description for a delightful little pasta. If you can't find orecchiette, medium-sized pasta shells are a good alternative. Stir this in with the fresh peas and some salty prosciutto, and you have a decadent addition to a meal in just a few minutes.

Yield: 4 servings

8 ounces orecchiette pasta

1½ teaspoons kosher salt

3 tablespoons olive oil

3 cloves garlic, minced or grated

1 cup peas, fresh or thawed

1 cup crème fraîche

¼ cup Parmesan cheese

6 slices prosciutto, shredded

12 small basil leaves, or 6 large ones roughly torn

In a large pot, bring water to a boil. Add pasta and a sprinkle of salt, cooking until pasta is al dente. While the pasta cooks, heat olive oil and garlic on medium heat for about 1 minute or until aromatic. Stir in the peas, then add the crème fraîche and salt. Bring to a simmer and continue to stir until heated through. Drain the pasta, reserving ⅓ cup of the cooking water, and add the pasta to the saucepan. Once the pasta is blended with the sauce, add the ⅓ cup of cooking water and cheese. Increase the heat to high and cook for 2 to 3 more minutes. Stir in the prosciutto and basil leaves.

"Life is a combination of magic and pasta."

—Federico Fellini

Colby Jack Macaroni and Cheese

All mac 'n' cheeses are not created equal, and this one comes out on top. The blend of sharp cheddar and colby jack cheeses makes for incomparable taste, and the added buttery breadcrumbs will have everyone eager for seconds.

Yield: 4–6 servings

4 cups medium shell macaroni

4 tablespoons butter

4 tablespoons flour

2 cups milk

Pinch of salt and freshly ground black pepper

6 cups sharp cheddar, shredded

½ cup sour cream

2 cups colby jack, cubed

½ cup Italian breadcrumbs

Preheat oven to 350°F. In a large pot, bring water to a boil. Add pasta and a sprinkle of salt, cooking until pasta is al dente. In a separate, large saucepan, create a roux by melting the butter and gradually adding in flour. Slowly add the milk, salt, and pepper on medium-low heat until thickened. Sprinkle in the cheddar while stirring continuously. Wait for cheese to melt before adding more. Reserve ½ cup for sprinkling at the end. Add sour cream. Mix in the pasta shells until evenly coated. Pour the shells into a large baking dish in layers. Add colby jack cheese to each layer. Finish with cheddar as the top layer and sprinkle breadcrumbs liberally. Bake for 45 to 55 minutes or until lightly browned.

Tip: Can also be cooked in small tapas dishes. Cut time in half.

Crispy Potato Pancakes

Crispy and savory, these potato pancakes are classic for a reason. Whether you are putting in a little extra sweat and shredding the potatoes with a box grater or just tossing them into the food processor, the result is a comforting side for holiday traditions and weeknight meals alike.

Yield: 6 servings

1 pound russet potatoes, peeled (2–3 potatoes)

1 small onion

1 large egg, lightly beaten

¼ teaspoon garlic powder

3 tablespoons matzo meal

Pinch of salt and freshly ground black pepper

½ cup vegetable oil

1 tablespoon chives, snipped

Chop the potatoes into large pieces and soak in water for an hour. Coarsely shred the potatoes and onion in a food processor. On a clean, dry kitchen towel, press out any excess moisture from the shredded potatoes and onions. Add the potatoes and onions to a large bowl and stir in the egg, garlic powder, matzo meal, salt, and pepper. Heat the vegetable oil in a large skillet on medium-high. In batches, drop heaping tablespoons of the potatoes onto the pan, flattening them into 3-inch pancakes with a spoon or spatula. Cook for 3 to 4 minutes on each side, or until the pancakes have lightly browned. Sprinkle with chives and serve with sour cream or apple sauce.

Spicy Jicama Fries

Jicama, sometimes known as a Mexican turnip, gets very little airtime on the vegetable scene. This underdog is great in salads, stir-fry, and even on a standard crudité platter, but these crunchy fries let jicama really shine. If you aren't big on spice but want to steer from a typical order of French fries, cook them plain and then sprinkle with a little salt and pepper.

Yield: 3 servings

1 medium jicama

1 tablespoon coconut or vegetable oil

½ teaspoon cumin

½ teaspoon turmeric

½ teaspoon garlic powder

Pinch of salt and freshly ground black pepper

Pinch of cayenne or chili powder

Preheat oven to 400°F. Peel the jicama and slice into thin-cut fries. Precook the jicama: Place the fries in a bowl with a tablespoon of water and microwave, covered with a damp paper towel, for 5 minutes. Drain the jicama and lightly pat dry. Toss the jicama fries with the oil and all of the spices. Arrange evenly on a parchment- or foil-lined baking sheet and bake for 40 minutes, or until they are lightly browned. Shift with a spatula or tongs at least once.

Thyme Sweet Potatoes

The crispy and sugary essence of sweet potatoes is a treat in itself, so this preparation takes a minimalist approach to let those flavors shine. With a little bit of spice from the red pepper and some fragrant thyme, these potatoes are like none other.

Yield: 6 servings

4 medium sweet potatoes, peeled and cut into cubes

3 tablespoons olive oil

4 large garlic cloves, minced

⅓ cup fresh thyme leaves

½ teaspoon kosher salt

½ teaspoon red pepper flakes

2 sprigs thyme for garnish

Preheat oven to 450°F. Toss ingredients together until sweet potatoes are evenly coated. Arrange on a parchment- or foil-lined baking sheet and roast for 45 minutes or until tender and lightly browned. Garnish with thyme sprigs.

"I hate people who are not serious about meals. It is so shallow of them."
—Oscar Wilde, *The Importance of Being Earnest*

Potato Gratin

A medley of simple ingredients that makes for a rich and creamy dish, these scalloped potatoes are more than what they seem. Whether you are taking all day to make rack of lamb or are whipping up something quickly, potato gratin can go with just about anything.

Yield: 6 servings

10 Idaho potatoes, peeled

2 tablespoons unsalted butter, softened

2 cloves garlic, minced

1½–2 cups half-and-half

Salt and freshly ground black pepper to taste

1 teaspoon nutmeg

½ cup heavy cream

½ cup Parmesan

Preheat the oven to 350°F. Slice potatoes to ⅛-inch thick using a sharp knife or mandolin. Using the butter, grease a shallow baking dish. Coat with half of minced garlic. In a saucepan, bring the half-and-half to a simmer over medium heat. Season with salt and pepper and add the rest of the garlic. Arrange the potatoes in one layer in the baking dish, overlapping like fish scales. Season this layer with salt, pepper, and nutmeg. Repeat this process in layers until all of the potatoes are gone or the dish is nearly filled. Pour the hot half-and-half over the potatoes, but do not fill above the top layer. Bake, covered, for 1 hour or until fork tender. Remove the foil and increase the heat to 415°F. Bake for another 8 to 10 minutes or until the potatoes are lightly browned. Pour cream over the top and sprinkle with Parmesan. Bake for another 15 minutes or until the top is lightly browned. Remove from the oven and let stand for 10 minutes and serve.

Tortilla Española

A traditional tapa or small plate in Spain, this egg-and-potato side dish is heartier than a quiche or frittata. Perfecting this recipe can take time, but the results speak for themselves. Serve in small bites or in wedges.

Yield: 4 servings

4 strands saffron

½ cup extra-virgin olive oil

2 large baking potatoes, peeled and thinly sliced crosswise

1 cup red onion, thinly sliced

5 large eggs

½ cup fresh cilantro, chopped

1 tablespoon fresh thyme

¼ teaspoon paprika

¼ teaspoon cumin

Pinch of salt and freshly ground black pepper

2 tablespoons olive oil

Preheat oven to 400°F. In an 8-inch skillet, heat saffron and olive oil over medium heat. Stir in potatoes and onion. Add more oil if necessary so that they are completely covered. Reduce the heat to medium-low and cook for 20 minutes. Remove contents from the skillet and drain out the oil. Combine potato mixture with eggs, cilantro, thyme, paprika, cumin, salt, and pepper. Mix well. Heat 2 tablespoons of olive oil over medium heat. Pour in mixture and press down evenly. Reduce heat and cook, uncovered, for 4 to 5 minutes or until the bottom has lightly browned. Cover with a ceramic plate and flip the tortilla onto the plate. Slide the tortilla, uncooked side down, back into the skillet. Cook for another 4 to 5 minutes. Remove from pan and serve in slices.

Tomatoes Provencal

These incredibly tasty stuffed tomatoes are inspired by Mediterranean cuisines that celebrate an array of fresh produce, herbs, and spices. This super-simple recipe can be thrown together for unexpected guests, making you look like the perfect host.

Yield: 8 servings

6 tomatoes, about 3 inches in diameter

Pinch of salt and freshly ground black pepper

1½ cups breadcrumbs

¼ cup scallions, minced

¼ cup basil leaves, minced

2 cloves garlic, minced

2 tablespoons parsley, minced

½ teaspoon oregano

1 teaspoon salt

½ cup grated Gruyère cheese

2 tablespoons extra-virgin olive oil

Preheat the oven to 400°F. Cut tomatoes in half crosswise and gently remove the seeds. Sprinkle with salt and pepper. In a bowl, mix the breadcrumbs, scallions, basil, garlic, parsley, oregano, and salt. Fill the tomatoes with the breadcrumb mixture. Bake for 15 minutes or until lightly browned and tender. Sprinkle with cheese and olive oil and brown in the oven for another minute.

"It's difficult to think anything but pleasant thoughts while eating a homegrown tomato."

—Lewis Grizzard

Baked Beans

Baked beans: an American staple for centuries. Whether you're prepping for a camping trip or enjoying the dog days of summer at a barbecue, now you can prepare this classic without the preservatives and artificial ingredients from the can.

Yield: 4–6 servings

4 cups dried navy beans, soaked overnight

1 medium onion, peeled and halved

4 whole cloves

8 ounces bacon or salt pork, cubed

¼ cup maple syrup

¼ cup dark molasses

2 teaspoons mustard powder

2 tablespoons dark rum

Pinch of salt and freshly ground black pepper

Combine ingredients in a 4-quart slow cooker. Turn on low and cook for 6 to 8 hours.

Popovers

Popovers are the savory American twist on the Yorkshire Pudding of England. It's a light fluffy roll, served sweet topped with whipped cream for a breakfast treat or with afternoon tea, or with meats for lunch or dinner. This easy recipe calls for a popover pan, but a muffin tin works perfectly, too!

Yield: 12 popovers

4 tablespoons (½ stick) unsalted butter, melted

6 eggs, lightly beaten

2 cups milk

2 cups all-purpose flour

1 teaspoon salt

Preheat an oven to 450°F. Grease the cups of a popover pan with butter or nonstick spray. Pour ½ teaspoon of melted butter into each well. Whisk the eggs and milk, followed by 2 tablespoons of melted butter. In a separate bowl, mix the flour and salt. Add in the egg mixture, stirring until smooth. Pour the batter into the popover wells and bake for 20 minutes. Reduce the heat to 325°F and cook for another 15 minutes. To remove popovers from pan, invert over a cooling rack. Repeat the cooking process for the remaining popover batter.

"All sorrows are less with bread. "

—Miguel de Cervantes, *Don Quixote*

Zucchini Casserole

Simple only in preparation but not in flavor, this zucchini casserole is more than the sum of its parts. Ripe with an array of fantastic fresh vegetables, fragrant herbs, and melted cheese, this piping hot casserole should make its way onto your table time and time again.

Yield: 6–8 servings

4 tablespoons butter

1 yellow onion, diced

2 cloves garlic, minced

1 large zucchini, sliced

1 large summer squash

1 cup mushrooms, sliced

1 cup sweet corn

1 tablespoon dried basil

1 teaspoon dried oregano

½ teaspoon salt

12 ounces shredded cheese, such as mozzarella or Fontina

3 eggs, beaten

Chives, chopped, for garnish

Preheat the oven to 375°F. Heat the butter in a large sauté pan over medium high. Stir in the onion, garlic, zucchini, squash, and mushrooms. Stir for a minute and then add the corn, sautéing for 5 to 7 minutes or until tender but not overcooked. Remove from the heat and mix in the basil, oregano, and salt. Add cheese and eggs and pour the mixture into a greased casserole dish or pie pan. Add extra zucchini slices on top and sprinkle with more cheese. Bake for 20 minutes, covered with foil. Remove foil and bake for another 5 to 10 minutes to brown. Sprinkle with chives before serving.

Cheesy Cauliflower

A casserole like no other, this dish is comforting, cheesy, and delicious. Enhanced by the fresh flavor and great texture of cauliflower, you will want to have it on your table again and again.

Yield: 4-6 servings

1 head cauliflower

1 summer squash, peeled

2 tablespoons butter

½ yellow onion, diced

1 clove garlic, minced

2 tablespoons flour

1½ cups milk

1½ cups sharp cheddar, shredded

½ cup Parmesan, grated

Pinch of salt and freshly ground black pepper

Preheat oven to 400°F. Break cauliflower into florets and chop squash into cubes. In a large pot, bring water to a boil over high heat. Cook cauliflower for 5 minutes. Strain cauliflower and place into a greased baking dish with squash. Melt butter and heat onion and garlic on medium heat for about 2 minutes or until aromatic and onions are translucent. Whisk in flour for 1 minute, and then slowly add in milk until evenly blended. Stir in and melt cheese, seasoning with salt and pepper. Pour cheese mixture over cauliflower and squash. Bake for 20 to 25 minutes or until cheese is bubbling and tops of cauliflower are browned.

> "The only time to eat diet food is while you're waiting for the steak to cook."
> —Julia Child

Rosemary Crispy Onions

Crunchy onion rings are an old favorite, but this recipe has a hint of something special. With a little bit of rosemary, these onion rings transform from an ordinary burger side to a delectable new favorite.

Yield: 4 servings

1 Vidalia onion, sliced crosswise into rings

2 cups buttermilk

4 cups olive oil

2 cups all-purpose flour, divided in half

2 tablespoons garlic salt

1 tablespoon fresh rosemary, finely chopped

1 tablespoon freshly ground black pepper

12 ounces lager-style beer

Soak onions in buttermilk for 30 minutes to an hour. Heat olive oil in medium saucepan to 375°F. Mix 1 cup flour, garlic salt, rosemary, and pepper in a bowl. Mix 1 cup flour and beer in a separate bowl. Dredge onions in the flour mixture and then the beer batter. Fry for 2 minutes in batches or until golden brown. Remove onions from the oil and set on a cooling rack or plate lined with paper towels to soak up excess oil.

Broccoli Quiche

Not just a breakfast food, this broccoli quiche is a hearty complement to a wide variety of meals. Serve it alongside roasted vegetables or green salad for a wholesome, satisfying feast.

Yield: 8 servings

1 tablespoon unsalted butter

2 cups medium yellow onion, diced

6 large eggs

¾ cup heavy cream

¾ pound broccoli florets, steamed

1 cup sharp cheddar, grated

Pinch of salt and freshly ground black pepper

Preheat oven to 375°F. Melt the butter in a skillet over medium heat. Add the onion and heat for about 5 to 7 minutes, or until golden. Whisk eggs and cream together in a large bowl. Add onion, broccoli, cheese, salt, and pepper to combine. Pour mixture into an oven-safe dish and cook for 40 to 45 minutes or until cooked through.

"I don't think any day is worth living without thinking about what you're going to eat next at all times."

—Nora Ephron

Index

A

Adobo Salsa, 16
Appetizers
    Adobo Salsa, 16
    Cheesy Garlic Artichoke Dip, 15
    Chicken Empanadas, 34
    Classic Hummus, 11
    Cucumbers & Tomatoes, 28
    Guacamole, 12
    Honeydew & Prosciutto, 27
    Mini Margherita Pizzas, 32
    Savory Pinwheels, 38
    Savory Sausage Puffs, 21
    Sesame Breadsticks, 36
    Spicy Fried Pickles, 23
    Spinach & Bacon Dip, 19
    Spinach Tart, 31
    Stuffed Mushrooms, 24
Artichokes
    Cheesy Garlic Artichoke Dip, 15
    Roasted Artichoke, 90
Arugula, Beet &, Salad, 64
Asparagus, Lemony, 72
Avocados
    Guacamole, 12

B

Bacon
    Baked Beans, 112
    Potato Skins, 54
    Savory Pinwheels, 38
    Spinach & Bacon Dip, 19
Baked Beans, 112
Balsamic Brussels Sprouts, 81
Basil
    Caprese Salad, 67
    Mini Margherita Pizzas, 32
    Orecchiette with Peas, 97
    Spinach Tart, 31
    Tomatoes Provencal, 111
    Vegetable Orzo Pasta Salad, 68
Beans. *See* Chickpeas; Navy beans
Beef broth
    Fiery Meatballs, 47
Beef Lettuce Wraps, 50
Beer
    Rosemary Crispy Onions, 120
Beet & Arugula Salad, 64
Bok Choy, 86
Broccoli
    Broccoli Quiche, 123
    Pine Nut Broccoli Rabe, 83
    Roasted Vegetable Medley, 79
    Vegetable Orzo Pasta Salad, 68
Broth. *See* Beef broth; Chicken broth
Brussels sprouts, Balsamic, 81

C

Cabbage. *See* Green cabbage
Caprese Salad, 67
Carrots
    Kohlrabi Slaw, 63
    Roasted Vegetable Medley, 79
    Walnut Carrots, 89
Cauliflower
    Cheesy Cauliflower, 119
    Roasted Vegetable Medley, 79
Cheddar cheese
    Broccoli Quiche, 123
    Cheesy Cauliflower, 119
    Chicken Empanadas, 34
    Colby Jack Macaroni and Cheese, 99
    Potato Skins, 54
    Spicy Sliders, 49
Cheese. *See* Cheddar cheese; Cream
    cheese; Feta cheese; Goat cheese;
    Gruyère cheese; Monterey jack
    cheese; Mozzarella cheese; Parme-
    san cheese; Velveeta cheese
Cheesy Cauliflower, 119
Cheesy Garlic Artichoke Dip, 15
Cherry tomatoes
    Adobo Salsa, 16
    Caprese Salad, 67
Chicken
    Chicken Empanadas, 34
    Classic Chicken Wings, 43
    Lime & Chili Chicken Kebabs, 44
Chicken broth
    Mushroom Risotto, 95
    Vegetable Orzo Pasta Salad, 68
Chickpeas
    Classic Hummus, 11
Chipotle peppers in adobo
    Adobo Salsa, 16
Classic Chicken Wings, 43
Classic Hummus, 11
Colby jack cheese
    Colby Jack Macaroni and Cheese, 99
Corn
    Grilled Mexican Corn, 84
    Zucchini Casserole, 117

Cous Cous Salad, 70
Crab Cakes, 58
Cranberries
    Cous Cous Salad, 70
Cream cheese
    Cheesy Garlic Artichoke Dip, 15
    Cucumbers & Tomatoes, 28
    Spinach & Bacon Dip, 19
Creamed Spinach, 76
Crispy Potato Pancakes, 101
Cucumbers & Tomatoes, 28

E
Eggs
    Broccoli Quiche, 123
    Popovers, 114

F
Feta cheese
    Vegetable Orzo Pasta Salad, 68
Fiery Meatballs, 47
Fire-roasted tomatoes
    Adobo Salsa, 16

G
Garlicky Green Beans, 75
Goat cheese
    Beet & Arugula Salad, 64
    Savory Pinwheels, 38
Grape tomatoes
    Vegetable Orzo Pasta Salad, 68
Green beans
    Garlicky Green Beans, 75
Green cabbage
    Kohlrabi Slaw, 63
Green onions
    Chicken Empanadas, 34
    Savory Pinwheels, 38
    Vegetable Orzo Pasta Salad, 68
Grilled Mexican Corn, 84
Ground beef
    Beef Lettuce Wraps, 50
    Spicy Sliders, 49
Gruyère cheese
    Tomatoes Provencal, 111
Guacamole, 12

H
Hearty Eats
    Beef Lettuce Wraps, 50
    Classic Chicken Wings, 43
    Crab Cakes, 58
    Fiery Meatballs, 47
    Lamb Lollipops, 53
    Lemon-Ginger Shrimp, 57

    Lime & Chili Chicken Kebabs, 44
    Potato Skins, 54
    Spicy Sliders, 49
Honeydew & Prosciutto, 27

J
Jalapeño peppers
    Adobo Salsa, 16
    Guacamole, 12
    Spinach & Bacon Dip, 19
Jicama, Spicy, Fries, 103

K
Kebabs, Lime & Chili Chicken, 44
Kohlrabi Slaw, 63

L
Lamb Lollipops, 53
Lemons
    Lemon-Ginger Shrimp, 57
    Lemony Asparagus, 72
Lettuce
    Beef Lettuce Wraps, 50
    Spicy Sliders, 49
Lime & Chili Chicken Kebabs, 44

M
Macaroni, Colby Jack, and Cheese, 99
Meatballs, Fiery, 47
Mini Margherita Pizzas, 32
Monterey jack cheese
    Chicken Empanadas, 34
Mozzarella cheese
    Caprese Salad, 67
    Mini Margherita Pizzas, 32
    Spinach Tart, 31
    Zucchini Casserole, 117
Mushrooms
    Creamed Spinach, 76
    Mushroom Risotto, 95
    Stuffed Mushrooms, 24
    Zucchini Casserole, 117

N
Navy beans
    Baked Beans, 112
Nuts. *See* Pine nuts; Walnuts

O
Olives
    Vegetable Orzo Pasta Salad, 68
Onions. *See also* Green onions; Red
    onions
    Baked Beans, 112
    Broccoli Quiche, 123

Onions (*continued*)
    Rosemary Crispy Onions, 121
    Zucchini Casserole, 117
Orecchiette with Peas, 97
Orzo, Vegetable, Pasta Salad, 68

P

Parmesan cheese
    Cheesy Cauliflower, 119
    Creamed Spinach, 76
    Grilled Mexican Corn, 84
    Lemony Asparagus, 72
    Mini Margherita Pizzas, 32
    Mushroom Risotto, 95
    Orecchiette with Peas, 97
    Potato Gratin, 107
    Potato Skins, 54
    Spinach Tart, 31
Pastas
    Colby Jack Macaroni and Cheese, 99
    Orecchiette with Peas, 97
Peas, Orecchiette with, 97
Peppers. *See* Chipotle peppers in adobo;
    Jalapeño peppers
Pickles, Spicy Fried, 23
Pie pastry
    Chicken Empanadas, 34
Pine Nut Broccoli Rabe, 83
Pine nuts
    Pine Nut Broccoli Rabe, 83
    Vegetable Orzo Pasta Salad, 68
Pizza, Mini Margherita, 32
Plum tomatoes
    Spicy Sliders, 49
Pomegranate
    Cous Cous Salad, 70
Popovers, 114
Potatoes
    Crispy Potato Pancakes, 101
    Potato Gratin, 107
    Potato Skins, 54
    Tortilla Española, 108
Prosciutto
    Honeydew & Prosciutto, 27
    Orecchiette with Peas, 97
Puff pastry
    Savory Pinwheels, 38
    Savory Sausage Puffs, 21

R

Red onions
    Roasted Vegetable Medley, 79
    Tortilla Española, 108
Risotto, Mushroom, 95
Roasted Artichoke, 90

Roasted Vegetable Medley, 79
Roma tomatoes
    Guacamole, 12
    Mini Margherita Pizzas, 32
Rosemary
    Lamb Lollipops, 53
    Rosemary Crispy Onions, 120

S

Salads
    Beet & Arugula Salad, 64
    Caprese Salad, 67
    Cous Cous Salad, 70
    Kohlrabi Slaw, 63
    Vegetable Orzo Pasta Salad,
        68–69
Sausage, Savory, Puffs, 21
Savory Pinwheels, 38
Savory Sausage Puffs, 21
Seafood
    Crab Cakes, 58
    Lemon-Ginger Shrimp, 57
Sesame Breadsticks, 36
Shrimp, Lemon-Ginger, 57
Sides
    Baked Beans, 112
    Balsamic Brussels Sprouts, 81
    Bok Choy, 86
    Broccoli Quiche, 123
    Cheesy Cauliflower, 119
    Creamed Spinach, 76
    Crispy Potato Pancakes, 101
    Garlicky Green Beans, 75
    Grilled Mexican Corn, 84
    Lemony Asparagus, 72
    Mushroom Risotto, 95
    Pine Nut Broccoli Rabe, 83
    Popovers, 114
    Potato Gratin, 107
    Roasted Artichoke, 90
    Roasted Vegetable Medley, 79
    Rosemary Crispy Onions, 120
    Spicy Jicama Fries, 103
    Thyme Sweet Potatoes, 104
    Tomatoes Provencal, 111
    Tortilla Española, 108
    Walnut Carrots, 89
    Zucchini Casserole, 117
Sliders, Spicy, 49
Sour cream
    Cheesy Garlic Artichoke Dip, 15
    Grilled Mexican Corn, 84
Spicy Fried Pickles, 23
Spicy Jicama Fries, 103
Spicy Sliders, 49

Spinach
   Creamed Spinach, 76
   Savory Pinwheels, 38
   Spinach & Bacon Dip, 19
   Spinach Tart, 31
Squash. *See* Summer squash
Stuffed Mushrooms, 24
Summer squash
   Cheesy Cauliflower, 119
   Zucchini Casserole, 117
Sun-dried tomatoes
   Cucumbers & Tomatoes, 28
Sweet Potatoes, Thyme, 104
Swiss chard
   Spinach Tart, 31

T
Thyme Sweet Potatoes, 104
Tomatoes. *See also* Cherry tomatoes;
      Fire-roasted tomatoes; Grape
tomatoes; Roma tomatoes;
      Sun-dried tomatoes
   Spinach & Bacon Dip, 19
   Spinach Tart, 31
   Tomatoes Provencal, 111
Tortilla Española, 108

V
Vegetable Orzo Pasta Salad,
      68–69
Velveeta cheese
   Spinach & Bacon Dip, 19

W
Walnuts
   Beet & Arugula Salad, 64
   Walnut Carrots, 89

Z
Zucchini Casserole, 117